WEIRD & WONDERFUL
SCIENCE EXPERIMENTS

VOLUME 2

COOL CREATIONS

MoonDance

This library edition published in 2018 by MoonDance Press,
an imprint of The Quarto Group
6 Orchard Road, Suite 100
Lake Forest, CA 92630

© 2017 Quarto Publishing Group USA Inc.
Text © 2017 Elizabeth Snoke Harris

Published by MoonDance Press,
a division of Quarto Publishing Group USA Inc.
All rights reserved. MoonDance is a registered trademark.

Illustrations by Jeff Albrecht Studios
Cover and interior design by Melissa Gerber

Distributed in the United States and Canada by
Lerner Publisher Services
241 First Avenue North
Minneapolis, MN 55401 U.S.A.
www.lernerbooks.com

Printed in USA
9 8 7 6 5 4 3 2 1

FSC
www.fsc.org
MIX
Paper from
responsible sources
FSC® C008080

Contents

Introduction

Have you ever wanted to...
Squeeze and squish your own homemade slime?
Write a secret message in invisible ink?
Skewer a balloon without popping it?

Great! You'll find easy-to-follow instructions for these and so many more cool creation experiments in this book. No matter whether you set out to make crystals, jewelry, or mischief, you are guaranteed to have fun!

Bottle Stopper, page 11

What's in this book?

- Many of the experiments can be done by kids all by themselves. That's right—no adult help needed. That means no grownups doing all the fun stuff while you watch. You can do lots of messy, cool, mind-blowing experiments all by yourself!

- All the supplies you need are probably already in your home. No fancy gadgets or doohickeys needed.

- Science is fun! There is no better boredom buster than a science experiment. You will learn something and astound and amaze your friends and family.

What are you waiting for?

Pick an experiment you are interested in, gather the materials, and get going! Make sure you check the safety instructions and find an adult to help if needed.

- **Supplies** includes all the stuff you need.

- **Do It!** has instructions for building and performing the experiment.

- **What's Happening?** Read the science behind the experiment.

- **What If?** includes ideas for making the experiment bigger, louder, longer, or just plain better.

Air Lift

Use the power of air to lift a heavy book off the table.

Supplies

Heavy book, Straw, Gallon-size resealable bag, Tape, Scissors

Do It!

1. Seal the bag and make sure there is no air inside. Cut a small hole through one side of the bag about an inch below the seal. Stick the straw in the hole and push it in a couple of inches. Use tape to seal the straw in the hole.

2. Lay the bag on a table so that the straw sticks out over the edge. Put the heavy book on top of the bag. Blow into the straw and watch the book rise off the tabletop.

What's Happening?

If you lift the book over the table, there is air between the book and the table. But if you drop the book, it falls and pushes the air out of the way as if it wasn't even there. Most of the time, you don't notice the air around you. We move through it almost effortlessly. But if you pack a bunch of air into a small space, like blowing up a balloon or a plastic bag, you can see the air molecules taking up space.

The bag between the book and the table holds the air in place. As you blow into the bag, the air becomes pressurized. The air molecules are pushed together and out equally in all directions. The bag pushes down on the table and up on the book, lifting it up!

What If?

What if you use a garbage bag? Can you lift a friend off the table? Have them sit on a flat piece of cardboard on top of the bag. Use duct tape to seal the open end of the bag and attach several straws so that other friends can help you blow up the bag.

Upside-down Glass of Water, Part 1

Air pushes against your body with a force of 15 pounds per square inch! Imagine a bowling ball pushing against every inch of your body. You are so used to this air pressure that you don't even notice it. Is air pressure enough to keep water in a glass, even if you turn it upside down?

Supplies

Drinking glass, Water, Index card

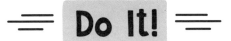 **Do It!**

1. Fill the glass at least half full of water.
2. Place the index card on top of the glass. Hold the glass with one hand and put your other hand flat over the index card. Quickly flip the glass upside down. Remove your hand from the index card. The water stays in the upside-down glass!

What's Happening?

The secret to this water trick is air. The air surrounds you and constantly bumps into you. There are also miles of air above you that are pulling downward onto you and the glass of water by gravity. All of this adds up to a force of about 15 pounds per square inch (psi) pushing on that glass of water from all directions.

Before you flip the glass upside down, the air pressure inside the glass and outside the glass are the same. However, during the flipping process, a tiny bit of water leaks out but no air gets in. This means the air left in the glass has a lower pressure than the air outside the glass. The outside air pushes up more than the inside air and the weight of the water push down and the water stays in the glass.

So, what keeps the card from falling off and letting the air in and the water out of the glass? The answer is surface tension and adhesion. Water has a positive end and a negative end. Because opposites attract, the water molecules line up with the opposite charges sticking together, making a sticky skin on the surface of the water. This sticky skin holds the water together. Scientists call this surface tension. The water sticks to itself but also to other stuff, such as the index card. The index card literally sticks to the surface of the water to keep air from getting in and water from getting out.

Upside-down Glass of Water, Part 2

What if you turn your glass upside down and take *off* the index card?

⹀ Do It! ⹀

Supplies

Mason jar with ring, Cheesecloth (or screen), Water, Index card

1. Cut a piece of cheesecloth a bit larger than the top of the mason jar. Lay it on the jar and screw the ring on top.
2. Fill the jar halfway with water. Hold the jar with one hand and put your other hand flat over the index card. Quickly flip the jar upside down. Remove your hand from the index card. Slowly slide the index card off the glass. Does the water stay in the jar? Tap your finger against the cheesecloth. Does the water still stay in the jar?

What's Happening?

Without the index card in place, surface tension is the main force holding the water in the jar. If you look at the cheesecloth while the jar is upside down, you'll see the water bulging through each hole. The water molecules stick to each other, forming a surface tension skin on the surface of the water. This sticky surface tension keeps the water from leaking through the holes.

Balloon in a Bottle

It's like a ship in a bottle … but with a balloon!

⹀ Do It! ⹀

Supplies

Plastic bottle, Balloon, Thumbtack, Nail

1. Push a balloon into the bottle and stretch the opening over the opening of the bottle. Blow into the balloon bottle. Can you blow up the balloon?
2. Use the thumbtack to poke a hole in the bottom of the bottle. With the nail, make the hole a little bigger. Blow into the balloon bottle. Can you blow up the balloon?
3. Blow up the balloon in the bottle again, and then put your finger over the hole in the bottom. What happens?
4. To trick a friend, offer to hold the bottle while they try to blow up the balloon. Keep your finger over the hole so the balloon won't blow up. When they give up, take your finger off the hole and blow up the balloon easily.

What's Happening?

It is impossible to blow up a balloon inside a bottle if there is nowhere for the air in the bottle to go. With a hole in the bottle, you can blow up the balloon and push the rest of the air in the bottle out of the hole.

Air Pressure Chop

There are over 70 miles of air pushing down on you right now. That is a lot of weight, but is it enough to break a ruler in half?

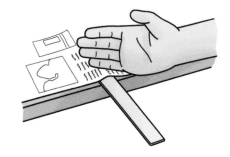

Supplies

Wooden ruler (without metal strip) or wooden paint stir stick, Newspaper, Tabletop

Do It!

1. Lay the ruler on the table so that a little less than half sticks out from the table. Chop the ruler hard and fast. Does the ruler move?

2. Lay the ruler on the table in the same way. Unfold two full sheets of newspaper and lay them over the ruler one on top of the other so that they completely cover the part of the ruler on the table. Smooth out the newspaper so there is no air between the paper and the table. Chop the ruler hard and fast. Does the ruler move now? Are you able to break the ruler? If not, try again and make sure the newspaper is smooth and you are striking the ruler very hard and fast.

What's Happening?

The first time you chopped the ruler without the newspaper, the ruler flipped off the table. The only force holding the ruler onto the table was gravity and the small amount of air pressure pushing on top of the ruler. Your chop easily overcame these forces. When you put the newspaper on top of the ruler, there is much more room for air pressure to push down. Air pushes down with a force of about 15 pounds for every square inch. Most newspapers are 23½ by 29½ inches. This means that, if there is no air under the paper, air pressure is pushing down on the newspaper with a force of over 10,000 pounds! However, you probably can't get all the air out from under the newspaper. When you chopped the ruler very fast, it quickly lifts the newspaper. The air does not have time to move into this space and a small vacuum is formed under the newspaper. This causes a suction effect when the high air pressure in the room pushes the newspaper back down.

What If?

What if you use just one piece of newspaper? Can you still break the ruler? What if you fold one piece in half? What is the smallest amount of paper (layers and size) you can use and still break the ruler?

Bernoulli Blower

Daniel Bernoulli was a Swiss mathematician and physicist in the early 1700s. He is best known for discovering that slow-moving fluids (such as air or water) have a higher pressure (push harder) than fast-moving fluids. This leads to some pretty cool phenomena, like this little toy made of string, paper, and a straw.

Supplies

Straw, Cardstock or construction paper, Hole punch, String, Tape, Scissors, Ruler, Markers (optional)

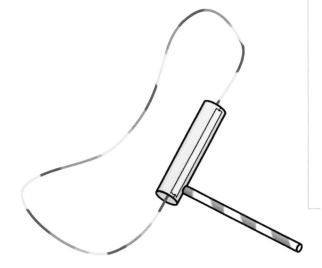

Do It!

1. Cut out a 3" x 2" rectangle from the cardstock. Roll the rectangle into a 3-inch-long tube and tape it together. Punch a hole about ½ inch from one end of the tube.

2. Cut a piece of string about 20 inches long. Thread the string through the tube and tie it so it makes a big loop. Cut off any extra string near the knot.

3. Cut a 4-inch piece of straw and stick it just up to the hole but not inside the tube. Blow hard and watch the string fly up into the air and go around through the tube. If you want, use the marker to decorate the tube and make stripes on the string so its motion is easier to see.

What's Happening?

According to Bernoulli's principle, fast-moving air has a lower pressure than slow-moving air. By blowing on the straw, you send fast-moving air up through the tube. The string gets carried along by the fast-moving air as it moves to the top of the tube. The slow-moving air outside of the tube pushes the string into the fast-moving stream coming out the top of the tube and lifts the string into the air. Because the string is a loop, it gets pulled back in the bottom of the tube and keeps going around.

Bernoulli's Water Gun

Daniel Bernoulli discovered that fast-moving air pushes less than slow-moving air. Little did he suspect that this discovery could be used to make a water gun!

Supplies

Straw, Glass of water, Scissors

═ Do It! ═

1. Cut the straw in half. Put one half in the glass of water and hold it so that only about an inch of straw sticks up out of the water.

2. Put the other straw in your mouth and blow hard at the top of the straw in the water. You may need to adjust the height of the straw and the angle at which you blow until a fine mist of water comes flying out of the straw in the water.

What's Happening?

Blowing across the top of the straw in the water causes low pressure above the straw. The still air in the straw and on top of the water has a higher pressure. This means the air in the straw pushes up and the air in the room pushes down on the water. All of this pushing sends water out of the straw. As soon as the water hits the fast-moving air, it breaks into tiny droplets that spray everywhere!

Bottle Crush

Flatten a water bottle using the strength of air pressure.

Supplies

Empty plastic water bottle, Hot water, Ice water, Large baking dish

═ Do It! ═

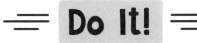

1. Fill the baking dish with ice water.

2. Pour ¼ cup of hot tap water into the water bottle and screw the cap on. Shake the bottle for 15 seconds. Take off the cap for just a couple of seconds and then screw it back on tightly.

3. Lay the bottle in the ice water and turn it around so that the ice water covers the entire bottle. Keep turning the bottle until it starts to crush in on itself.

What's Happening?

When you shake the hot water in the bottle, you are heating up the air inside. Hot air expands and pushes out on the bottle. When you take the lid off the bottle, even just for a few seconds, the hot air pushes out of the bottle, leaving less air inside. When you put the bottle in the ice water, the air inside cools very quickly. The cold air contracts, causing less pressure inside the bottle. The higher air pressure outside pushes on the bottle, causing it to flatten!

Bottle Stopper

Watch as a table tennis ball appears to defy gravity!

Supplies

Table tennis ball, Plastic drink bottle, Water

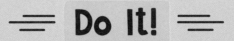
Do It!

1. Fill the bottle to the top with water.
2. Place the ball on top of the bottle. Slowly pick up the bottle and turn it upside down. Do NOT touch the ball while you do this. The ball and the water stay in the bottle!

What's Happening?

We hardly ever notice that air is all around us. Yet the air near the surface of the earth, where we are, is pushing on us and everything else with a force of about 15 pounds per square inch. This experiment works because of the round shape of the ball. It has a large surface area, which means that a lot more air pressure is pushing on it than a flat piece of paper of the same round size. As long as the force from air pressure on the ball is greater than the weight of the water in the bottle, it will stay in place!

Cups on a Balloon

Glue and tape aren't the only ways to make things stick together.

Do It!

1. Dip the top of one cup into the water.
2. Blow up the balloon to the size of a tennis ball. Have your friend hold the cup under the bottom of the balloon. Continue to blow up the balloon so that some of it stays in the cup. Once the balloon is blown up all the way, let go of the cup. Does the cup stick to the balloon?
3. Try again using two cups dipped in water. When the balloon is tennis-ball size, have your friend hold the cups onto the sides of the balloon. When the balloon is fully inflated, do the cups stay on the balloon?

Supplies

Balloons, Disposable cups, Bowl of water, Friend

What's Happening?

When you stick a cup on a balloon, the balloon pushes some of the air out of the cup. As you continue to blow up the balloon, the balloon flattens and takes up less room in the cup. This means there is more room for the air that was left in the cup and causes lower pressure inside the cup. The higher-pressure air outside pushes the cup onto the balloon. Dipping the cup in the water helps prevent air from leaking into the cup.

Floating Candle

Do tea light candles float? Find out in this illuminating experiment!

ADULT NEEDED

Supplies

Tea light candle, Pie pan, Water, Food coloring, Lighter or match, Clear drinking glass

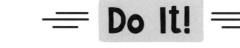

Do It!

1. Pour ½ inch of water into the pan, but not any deeper than your candle is tall. Add food coloring to make the water easier to see.
2. Place the candle in the middle of the pan and light it. Let the candle burn for a few seconds, and then place the drinking glass upside down over the candle. What happens to the flame and the water in the pan?

What's Happening?

The water level changes suddenly because of heat and air pressure. While the candle is burning, it heats the air inside the glass. The hotter air expands, pushing against the glass with a higher air pressure. When the candle uses up all the fuel in the glass and goes out, the air in the glass cools suddenly. The cooling air contracts and lowers the air pressure inside the glass. The higher air pressure in the room pushes water into the lower-pressure glass so that the pressure on both sides is equal.

Flying Cups

Levitate a cup using the power of your breath.

Do It!

1. Place one cup inside the other.
2. Hold the cups in front of your face, level with your mouth. Take a deep breath and blow hard. What happens to the inside cup? Now blow a little more gently. Can you make one cup float inside the other?

Supplies

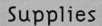

2 plastic cups

What's Happening?

Still air pushes more than moving air. Scientists call this the Bernoulli Principle. This principle explains everything from why airplanes fly to why the shower curtain sometimes attacks you when you take a hot shower. In this experiment, it explains why the inside cup goes flying.

When you put one cup inside the other, there's a small amount of air in the bottom between the cups. This air is not moving, and neither is the air at the top of the cups. When you blow across the rims of the cups, the air moves around the top of the cup. Now the air at the top of the cups is moving and not pushing down as hard as it used to, so the air inside the outside cup pushes the top cup out.

Jumping Coin

Putting an empty bottle in the freezer with a coin for a lid can lead to some explosive results!

Supplies

Empty soda bottle (plastic or glass), Coin (large enough to cover the top of the bottle), Freezer, Paper towel, Water

═ Do It! ═

1. Take the top off the bottle and place it in the freezer for at least an hour until it is cold.

2. Cut out a round piece of paper towel the same size as the coin. Wet the paper towel completely. Without taking the bottle out of the freezer, place the paper towel and the coin over the top of the bottle so that the opening is completely covered. Close the freezer and wait another 30 minutes until the paper towel is completely frozen.

3. Take the bottle out of the freezer and use your hands to warm up the bottle. Make sure the opening is pointed away from you, other people, and anything that could break. After about a minute, the coin will shoot off the bottle!

What's Happening?

When you put the empty bottle in the freezer without a cover, the bottle and the air inside both get very cold. Air contracts and takes up less space when it is cold. Because the bottle is open, more air goes into the cold bottle than was in the warm bottle. Putting the wet paper towel and coin on top of the bottle seals the bottle so no air can come in or out. (The coin is too bumpy to seal it completely, so the wet paper towel ensures that the bottle is completely sealed.) When you take the bottle out of the freezer and warm it up, the air expands again and takes up more space. Because extra air went into the cold bottle, there is more air than the warm bottle can hold, and it pushes the coin off the top.

What If?

What if you use a smaller or larger bottle? What if you put the frozen bottle in hot water to warm it up even quicker? What can you change to make the coin shoot higher and more quickly?

Magnus Flyer

This simple flyer uses the same science that pitchers use to throw a curve ball.

Supplies

2 Styrofoam cups, Tape, String, Rubber band, Markers (optional)

≡ Do It! ≡

1. Place one cup on the table upside down and the other on top of the first right-side up so that the bottoms are together. Wrap tape around the cups to hold them together. You can decorate the cups with markers, if you like. The decorations make it easier to see the spinning motion.

2. Cut a piece of string about 30 inches long. Tie one end of the string to the rubber band to make the launcher.

3. Wrap the string around the center of the flyer, where the cups are taped together. Stretch out the rubber band at the end of the string so that it goes once around the flier, as well. Hold the flyer with one hand so that the rubber band comes out underneath the flyer. Stretch out the rubber band away from you and pull the flyer toward your face. Release the flyer. Watch it spin and glide!

What's Happening?

When you release the launcher, the cups spin in the air. If you look carefully, the flyer is moving away from you, but the cups are spinning toward you. This is called bottom spin. This bottom spin causes whirlpools of air behind the cups, which pushes the flier up and forward. Scientists call this the Magnus Effect. In baseball, the Magnus Effect is used to throw curve balls, but instead of topspin, the pitcher adds a sidespin, which causes the ball to turn or curve sideways.

What If?

What if you use smaller or larger Styrofoam cups? What size cups gives the longest and highest flight?

Does the length of the string in the launcher matter? Try using long rubber bands in a chain instead of the string. Which launcher gives the longest flight? What happens if you wrap the launcher around the flier in the other direction?

Cup Jump

Can you make a table tennis ball jump without touching it?

Table tennis ball, 2 cups

Do It!

1. Place the ball in one cup and put the empty cup right behind it.
2. Gently blow across the top of the first cup and slightly down toward the far side of the ball. What does the ball do? Give a big, strong blow and watch it jump from one cup into the other. It may take some practice to get the angle and strength of the blow just right to make the ball jump directly into the other cup.

What's Happening?

When you blow across the top of the cup and down on the far side of the ball, you create low pressure in these areas. The air under the ball and closer to you is not moving and has a greater pressure, which pushes the ball up and into the other cup.

Floating Ball

Make a ball float with the power of science!

Supplies

Hair dryer, Table tennis ball

Do It!

1. Turn the hair dryer on its highest setting and point it straight up. Place the ball in the flow of air. What does the ball do?
2. Slowly tilt the hair dryer at an angle. How far can you tilt the hair dryer before the ball falls?
3. Gently move the hair dryer straight up and down. What does the ball do now?

What's Happening?

The fast-moving air coming out of the hair dryer has a much lower pressure than the still air in the room around it. The stream of fast-moving air pushes the ball up. Every time it starts to move out of this stream of fast air, the high pressure from the still air in the room pushes it back. Tilt the hair dryer until the weight of the ball is greater than the high pressure pushing upward, and the ball falls.

What If?

Can you float more than one ball at a time with the hair dryer? What other objects can you float? Try a balloon or an empty toilet paper tube.

Ball in the Funnel

Can you blow a ball out of a funnel?

Supplies

Funnel,
Table tennis ball

1. Place the small end of the funnel in your mouth. Tilt your head back so the large end is pointed up.

2. Place the ball in the funnel. Blow as hard as you can. Does the ball come out? Try it again, but this time, while you're blowing, tilt your head forward so the large end of the funnel points down. Does the ball come out of the funnel while you are blowing?

What's Happening?

It turns out that blowing into the funnel keeps the ball inside the funnel. When you blow, the fast-moving air creates low pressure under and around the ball. The high pressure in the room pushes the ball into the funnel. The harder you blow, the more the ball sticks in the funnel!

Shoot the Breeze

The next three experiments use the power of air to create a cannon.

Basic Air Cannon

Use a simple cardboard box to shoot air all the way across the room!

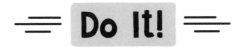

Supplies

Large box (at least
12 inches long and
12 inches wide),
Tape, Scissors,
Styrofoam Cups

1. If your box has any loose flaps, tape them in place so you have a sealed box. Cut a hole about 4 inches across on a small end of the box.

2. Stack a pyramid of Styrofoam cups as a target for your cannon.

3. Stand about 3 feet away from the cup pyramid. Aim the open end of the cannon at the cups. To shoot the cannon, take both hands and slam them on the sides of the box. An air cannonball will knock over the cups! Keep moving back to see how far away you can use the cannon to knock over the cups.

Portable Air Cannon

This air cannon is small enough to fit in your backpack.

Supplies

Plastic yogurt cup, Balloon, Scissors, Tape, Toilet paper

Do It!

1. Cut a small, round hole in the middle of the bottom of the yogurt container.

2. Stretch the balloon by blowing it up and letting the air back out. Cut the open end off the balloon and stretch the top over the large opening of the yogurt container. Tape the balloon in place.

3. To shoot the cannon, pull back on the balloon, and then release it so that it snaps back onto the yogurt cup. Air will shoot out of the small hole. Tape long strips of toilet paper from the top of a doorway to use as a target for your cannon. How far away can you stand and make the toilet paper move?

Smoke Rings

Use smoke to see just what comes out of the air cannon.

ADULT NEEDED

Supplies

Incense stick, Lighter, Air cannon (either the basic or portable version)

Do It!

1. Light the end of the incense stick and let it burn for two seconds. Blow it out and stick the smoking end inside your air cannon. Cover the opening with your hands so the smoke doesn't escape. When the cannon is full of smoke, take out the incense stick and put it aside.

2. Shoot the air cannon. Do you see the smoke rings?

3. Now that you can see the air coming out of your air cannon, you can measure its speed. Stand 6 feet away from a target and time how long it takes the smoke ring to get there. Use a calculator to divide the distance by the time to get the speed.

What's Happening?

When you shoot an air cannon, the air inside pushes out through the hole. As this air comes out, it pushes the air that was already there out of the way, creating a twisting doughnut of air called a toroidal vortex. A vortex describes the twisting of a fluid. You have probably seen a vortex when you drain the bathtub. Vortices are special because the motion is stable and doesn't need any help to keep its shape. The toroidal vortex from your air cannon is so stable, it will travel across the room before it falls apart. When you add smoke to your cannon, you see exactly how far it goes!

Big Bag Blow-up

How many breaths do you think it would take to blow up a garbage bag? Can you blow up the bag with just ONE breath?

Supplies

Large garbage bag

Do It!

1. Gather the open end of the garbage bag and blow air into it just like you would a balloon. How many breaths does it take to fill the bag with air?

2. Squeeze the air out of the bag. Hold the bag open about a foot in front of your mouth. Take a deep breath and blow as hard and long as you can into the bag. Are you able to blow up the bag with just one breath?

What's Happening?

When you hold the bag close to your mouth and blow, the only air going into the bag is the air from your lungs. It takes a LOT of breaths to fill the bag. When you hold the opening of the bag farther away and blow air out of your mouth, it moves faster than the air in the rest of the room. Still-moving air has more pressure, or pushes harder, than fast-moving air. As the fast-moving air moves into the bag, the higher-pressure still air in the room pushes into the bag and fills it quickly!

On-Off Fountain

Turn this water fountain on and off with just the tip of your finger.

Do It!

Supplies

Small water bottle, Bucket, Water, Straw, Modeling clay, Thumbtack

1. Poke a hole in the bottom of the plastic bottle. Cut the straw in half. Wrap clay around the middle of the piece of straw and stick the straw into the top of the bottle. Use the clay to seal the straw into the bottle.

2. Fill the bucket with water. Stick the bottle into the water, straw-end first, so that almost all the bottle is under water. Water should come bubbling up through the straw inside the bottle like a fountain. Put your finger over the hole in the bottom of the bottle (sticking out of the water). What happens to the fountain? Take your finger off the hole. What happens now?

What's Happening?

When you push an empty bottle full of air down under water, the water pushes on the air trapped in the bottle, causing high air pressure inside the bottle. The air pushes out of the hole as the water pushes up through the straw. When you close the hole, the water flows until the pressure in the bottle is the same as that in the water, and then the fountain stops flowing. Remove your finger and the fountain flows again.

Fountain Inside a Bottle

Watch as a fountain forms in a bottle!

Supplies

Glass soda bottle, Modeling clay, Straw, Bowl, Hot water, Cold water, Ice, Food coloring

Do It!

1. Depending on the size of your bottle, you might need to cut the straw. The straw should be about 3 inches shorter than your bottle. Wrap modeling clay around the straw about an inch from the end.

2. Pour hot water into the soda bottle. Hot water from the faucet will work fine, but hotter water will make the fountain rise higher. Pour cold water into the bowl, along with a couple of ice cubes and a few drops of food coloring.

3. Quickly pour the hot water out of the bottle and put the straw into the bottle. Use the modeling clay to seal the straw on the bottle with the long end inside the bottle. Immediately turn the bottle upside down in the bowl of cold colored water. Watch the fountain inside the bottle!

What's Happening?

The hot water in the bottle is used to heat up the bottle and the air inside of it. Hot air molecules move faster and farther apart than cool air, so there is less air inside the hot bottle than when it was cool. When you put the straw in the bottle and seal it with clay, it is difficult for the cooler air to get into the bottle. Once the bottle is upside down in the cold water, the air inside cools and contracts. This creates low pressure inside the bottle, and the cold water pushes up the straw and sprays into the bottle.

Fountain Outside a Bottle

Fountains don't always need to be inside bottles to work.

Supplies

2-liter soda bottle, Balloon, Bendable straw, Modeling clay, Pen, Tray

Do It!

1. Poke a hole in the middle of the side of the bottle. Push the pen through to make a round hole. Stick the straw through the hole so that the bottom of the straw is near the bottom of the bottle. The bendable part of the straw should be outside the bottle and bend upward. Use the clay to seal the hole around the straw.

2. Fill the bottle with water and place it in the tray to catch the water. Blow up the balloon and put it on the top of the bottle. Watch the fountain flow outside the bottle!

What's Happening?

A balloon full of air has very high air pressure. If you let go of the balloon before tying it off, it pushes out on the water so that it flows out through the straw.

In the Lab

Unleash your inner mad scientist and make bubbles, crystals, plastic, and slime!

Antibubbles

What is a bubble that's inside-out and under water?
An antibubble!

Supplies

Tall, clear jar or vase; Water; Dish soap; Spoon; Sugar; Pipette or small syringe; Small bowl

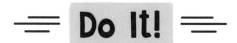

Do It!

1. Fill the jar ¾ full of water. Add two squirts of dish soap and gently mix the soap in with a spoon. Try not to make any bubbles.

2. Pour a tablespoon or more of sugar into the jar. The amount depends on the size of your jar. You want a small layer of sugar on the bottom.

3. Fill the small bowl with water. Gently mix in one squirt of dish soap and a teaspoon of sugar.

4. Fill the pipette or syringe with the mixture in the bowl. Hold the tip of the syringe close, but just above the top surface of the water in the jar. Carefully release one drop at a time. Some of the water drops will briefly sit on the surface of the water before popping. With a little practice, you will be able to get drops that go under the surface of the water and slowly sink down to hover in the middle of the jar or rest on the sugar at the bottom. These are antibubbles!

5. If you cannot get the drops to go down into the water, add a little more dish soap and gently stir it in without disturbing the sugar at the bottom.

What's Happening?

A regular bubble is a drop of air surrounded by a shell of soap and water floating in the air. An antibubble is a drop of water surrounded by a shell of air floating in the water. To make an antibubble, you first must make the water less sticky. Water sticks to itself so strongly that it makes a skin on the top surface. Adding soap makes the water less sticky, which allows a water drop surrounded by air to break through the skin, also called surface tension. Sugar is added to water drops to make them heavier than water so that they sink instead of rising to the top and popping.

What If?

What if you add food coloring to the water in the bowl? Color will help you better see the antibubble and what happens to it when it pops.

Long-lasting Bubbles

A few tricks will make your bubbles stick around longer.

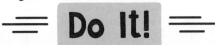

Do It!

Supplies

Dish soap, Distilled water, Corn syrup, Bowl, Measuring cup, Measuring spoon, Bubble wand or straw

1. In a bowl, mix 1 cup of water with ¼ cup of dish soap. Let the mixture sit for an hour.

2. Dip the bubble wand or straw into the bubble solution and blow some bubbles. Use the stopwatch to time how long the bubbles last before they pop.

3. Gently mix 1 tablespoon of corn syrup into the bubble solution. Use the bubble wand or straw to blow bubbles with the new solution. Do the bubbles last longer?

What's Happening?

A bubble is made of two layers of soap with water in between. The soap and water stick together, and when you blow a bubble, they stretch out and hold the air inside. When the water in the middle evaporates or the bubble is broken, it pops. Adding corn syrup creates thicker soap layers so the water doesn't evaporate as quickly and the bubble is harder to break. Using distilled water and letting the solution sit for an hour prevents impurities and gas bubbles in the solution that can cause your bubbles to pop. The result is longer-lasting bubbles!

Bouncing Bubbles

These bubbles will bounce off your hands!

Do It!

Supplies

Dish soap, Distilled water, Glycerin, Refrigerator, Bowl, Measuring cup, Measuring spoon, Bubble wand or straw, Knit cotton glove or a clean sock

1. In a bowl, mix 1 cup of water with ¼ cup of dish soap. Gently mix 1 tablespoon of glycerin into the bubble solution. Let the mixture sit in the refrigerator for at least 24 hours.

2. Put on a glove. With the other hand, use the bubble wand or straw to blow a bubble onto your gloved hand. Gently bounce the bubble around on your hand!

What's Happening?

The glycerin in the bubble solution makes the soap layers thicker, stronger, and less likely to pop. By cooling the solution, the water between the soap layers takes longer to evaporate, which also makes the bubbles harder to pop. The bubbles are strong enough to hold and bounce!

What If?

What if you don't cool your solution in the refrigerator? How does this affect the bounciness of the bubbles?

Giant Bubbles

Bubbles come in all sizes, but giant ones are always more fun!

Supplies

Bubble solution, 2 sticks (from outside or bamboo skewers), Cotton string, 2 rubber bands, Washer or nut, Bucket

═ Do It! ═

1. Cut an 18-inch-long piece of string. Tie the ends of the string to the end of each stick.

2. Cut a 36-inch-long piece of string. Thread the string through the washer. Tie these ends to the same ends of the sticks that you tied the other string. Wrap a rubber band several times around the sticks over the strings to hold them in place.

3. Pour 1 inch of bubble solution into the bucket. Hold the sticks together and dip the entire string into the bubble solution. Pull the string straight up and keep the sticks together. Hold the sticks high and slowly pull the sticks apart as you walk backward. A giant bubble will form as the air pushes through the bubble solution between the strings.

What's Happening?

Water is sticky. It sticks to almost everything, but it sticks to itself more. Water alone is too sticky to make bubbles. A mixture of soap and water — the basics of a bubble solution — is just sticky enough but not too sticky that it stretches out into a thin film. The bubble solution sticks to the cotton string, so when you pull it apart, you get a very thin sheet of bubble solution. Even the slightest breeze will stretch that sheet outward until it makes a giant, round bubble.

What If?

What if you make a bubble big enough to hold a person? Pour bubble solution into a kiddie pool and throw in a hula hoop. Have a friend stand in the center of the hula hoop, and then pull it slowly upward. The bubble solution will stick to the hoop as you pull it up, making a bubble around your friend!

Dry Ice Bubbles

These bubbles are spooky-looking! For safety's sake, ask a grown-up to help you with the dry ice.

ADULT NEEDED

Supplies

Wide-mouth jar, Rubber hose, Funnel (big enough to cover the top of the jar), Bubble solution (the Bouncing Bubbles recipe is recommended), Dry ice (from the grocery store or an ice cream shop), Tongs or leather gloves, Water, Cotton knit gloves

Do It!

1. Fill the jar about halfway with warm water.
2. Stick the end of the funnel onto one end of the rubber hose.
3. Ask an adult to put a few pieces of dry ice into the jar. Make sure they wear leather gloves or use tongs to pick up the dry ice. DO NOT touch dry ice with your bare hands.
4. Hold the funnel over the top of the jar so that the "smoke" flows into the rubber hose. Dip the other end of the hose into the bubble solution. Soon you will see smoke-filled bubbles dropping off the end of the hose. Put on the cotton gloves if you want to hold and bounce the smoky bubbles.

What's Happening?

Dry ice is frozen carbon dioxide. At room temperature, carbon dioxide is a gas, but if you cool that gas down to -110°F, it becomes solid. Dry ice is so cold that touching it immediately burns the skin. When you add dry ice to warm water, it warms up so quickly that it changes straight from the solid state to the gas state, called sublimation. The smoke that you see is carbon dioxide mixed with water as a gas, like your smoke-like breath on a very cold day.

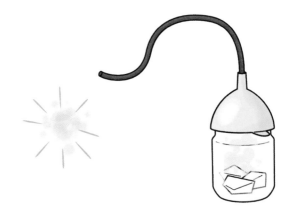

What If?

What if you put food coloring in the water? Can you make colored "smoke" in the bubbles?

Bubbles Inside Bubbles

Why create one bubble when you can make many?

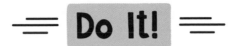

Do It!

1. Spread bubble solution on the flat surface with your hands.
2. Dip one end of the straw in the solution and hold it an inch above the soapy surface. Blow into the straw to make a large half bubble.
3. Dip your straw in the solution and stick it through the center of the bubble, an inch above the soapy surface. Blow into the straw to make another bubble slightly smaller than the first. It's a bubble within a bubble! Can you add a third bubble inside the second bubble?

Supplies

Bubble solution, Straw, Flat surface

What's Happening?

The soap and water in the bubble solution stick together. When you blow a bubble, it stretches out and holds the air on the soapy surface. Because the surface and straw are covered with solution, they become part of the bubble instead of popping it. When you blow a bubble inside a bubble, the outer bubble gets a little bigger. This is because you are blowing more air inside both bubbles.

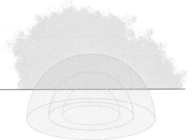

Square Bubbles

How do you create cubed bubbles?

Do It!

Supplies

7 straws, 7 12-inch pipe cleaners, Scissors, Bubble solution, Bucket

1. Bend the end of a pipe cleaner into a square wand. Dip it into the solution and blow. Does the wand make a square bubble?
2. Cut six straws and six pipe cleaners in half. Twist the ends of three pipe cleaners together. Bend them apart to make a pyramid. Twist the other pipe cleaners to make four pyramids.
3. Slide the straws over the pipe cleaners. Create a cube with the pyramids. Twist the ends to hold them together.
4. Pour solution into the bucket. Dip the cube completely into the solution. Slowly pull it out. What shape are the bubbles? Shake the cube gently and see how the shape changes. Use a straw to blow a bubble into the center of the cube. What shape is the bubble?

What's Happening?

Bubbles are round because a sphere requires only a little bubble solution to hold a lot of air. The cube wand changes that. The bubble solution sticks to the sides of the wand and stretches the shortest distance between sides. Blow a bubble in the middle, and the other bubbles in the cube push on it to create a square.

How Much Can You Blow?

Are you full of hot air? This experiment can help you find out.

Supplies

Bubble solution, Straw, Plastic garbage bag, Ruler, Calculator

═ Do It! ═

1. Lay the garbage bag flat on a table or other flat surface. Make sure the bag is smooth with very few wrinkles.

2. Pour a tiny amount of bubble solution on the bag and spread it out. Keep your ruler out and ready.

3. Dip the straw in the bubble solution and hold it just above the center of the bag. Take a deep breath and blow as much air as you possibly can out of your lungs to create a large bubble on the bag.

4. Use a ruler to quickly measure the diameter (width) of the bubble. If the bubble pops, measure the soapy outline of the bubble on the bag. Use a calculator to measure the volume of air in liters inside the bubble. If you measured in inches: diameter x diameter x diameter x .00429 = volume in liters. If you measured in centimeters: diameter x diameter x diameter x .000262 = volume in liters.

5. Repeat the process by breathing out normally as you blow up the bubble. Repeat again by breathing in normally, exhaling normally, and then blowing a bubble with all the air left in your lungs. Measure the diameter of both these bubbles and calculate the volume. A bubble 20 cm (8 inches) in diameter is about the same size as a 2-liter soda bottle!

What's Happening?

Lung capacity is the amount of air you can hold in your lungs. There are three types of lung capacity. Vital capacity is all the air your lungs can hold. Tidal volume is the air you normally have in your lungs. Expiratory reserve is the air you have left in your lungs after a normal breath. Which of these volumes was greatest, and which was smallest? Many factors affect your lung capacity, including your height, weight, and whether you live at high or low altitude.

To calculate the amount of air in the bubble, we used the equation for the volume of a sphere ($4/3 \pi$ (radius)^3), divided by 2 because there is only half a sphere on the garbage bag, adjusted for the units used and for the diameter of the sphere being twice the radius.

Alum Crystals

When you want large and impressive crystals, alum is your friend.

Supplies

Alum (find it in the spice section), Water, Measuring cup, 2 jars or cups, Mixing spoon, Pencil, Fishing line, Coffee filter

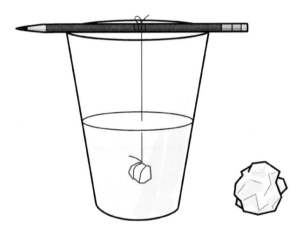

═ Do It! ═

1. Pour ½ cup of hot tap water into one of the jars. Stir in a small amount of alum at a time until no more alum will dissolve. Place a coffee filter over the jar and let it sit overnight.

2. Pour the alum water into the other jar. You will see some small crystals on the bottom of the first jar. Pour out the crystals and choose the biggest one.

3. Cut a piece of fishing line a few inches longer than the jar is tall. Tie one end around the crystal. Tie the other end around the middle of a pencil. Hang the seed crystal inside the jar by resting the pencil across the top of the jar. The crystal should hang in the middle of the alum water. If the line is too long, just turn the pencil so it wraps around to shorten the line. Place the jar in a warm, dry place and lay the coffee filter on top to keep dust out.

4. Check on the crystal several times each day to watch it grow. If you notice crystals on the bottom or sides of the jar, pour the alum water into a new, clean jar and move the crystal too. The other crystals in the jar will also act as seeds and slow down the growth of the crystal on the line. How large can you get the alum crystal to grow?

What's Happening?

Scientists call this process of growing crystals "nucleation." In nucleation, a couple of alum molecules in the water stick together and fall to the bottom of the jar. Soon, other alum molecules join the first two and a crystal starts to grow. This crystal becomes a seed for more crystals to grow. If you take the other seed crystals out of the jar, the only place for the molecules to stick is the seed crystal on the string. The larger this crystal gets, the faster it will grow because there is more room for the alum molecules in the water to join on.

Crystal Garden

Create your own garden of brilliantly colored crystal flowers.

Supplies

2 plastic containers, Charcoal briquettes, Water, Ammonia, Liquid bluing, Salt, Measuring spoon, Mixing spoon, Food coloring

═ Do It! ═

1. Cover the bottom of one of the plastic containers with charcoal.
2. In the other container, mix 4 tablespoons each of salt, water, and liquid bluing, and 1 tablespoon of ammonia.
3. Pour the mixture over the charcoal. Add drops of food coloring to the charcoal.
4. Place the container in a warm, dry spot. Crystals will form in a few hours.
5. To grow more crystals, add more liquid mixture as it evaporates. Pour the solution carefully down the side of the container, avoiding the crystals. If you get ammonia or bluing on your hands, wash it off immediately.

What's Happening?

Each ingredient plays a role in creating the crystals in the garden. The water and ammonia dissolve the bluing and salt. They carry the bluing and salt up through the holes in the charcoal. Ammonia helps the water evaporate quicker so smaller crystals are formed. Bluing is made of tiny particles suspended in the liquid. Salt sticks to those particles to form crystals.

Crystal Snowflakes

These snowflakes won't melt!

═ Do It! ═

1. Fill the jar ¾ full of hot tap water. Stir in several spoonfuls of Borax until it won't dissolve anymore.
2. Cut the pipe cleaner into three equal pieces. Twist the pieces together in the center and shape them into a star.
3. Cut a piece of string that's half as tall as the jar. Tie one end of the string to the pipe cleaner. Tie the other end to the pencil.
4. Lower the pipe cleaner into the jar. Rest the pencil across the top to hold it in place. The pipe cleaner should be submerged but not touching the bottom.
5. Place the jar in a cool spot. After 24 hours, pull your crystal snowflake out of the jar.

Supplies

Borax soap, Water, Tall jar, Mixing spoon, Pencil, String, Pipe cleaner, Scissors

What's Happening?

When you pour Borax into water, it dissolves into tiny particles that are suspended in the water. Hot water holds more Borax particles than cold water, and more particles mean more crystals. As the water cools, the Borax falls out of suspension and sticks to other Borax particles, forming crystals.

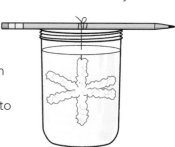

Eggshell Geodes

Geodes usually take centuries to form. You can make one in just a couple of days!

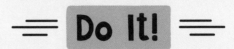

Supplies

Large eggshell, White glue, Small paintbrush, Jar, Water, Alum, Measuring spoon, Measuring cup, Food coloring, Mixing spoon, Paper towel

1. Clean and dry the eggshell.
2. Pour two drops of glue into the eggshell and paint it all over the inside surface.
3. Pour alum into the shell, turning it around so that the alum sticks to the glue and the inside is covered. Let it dry overnight.
4. In a jar, mix 1 cup of hot tap water, 6 tablespoons of alum, and 15 drops of food coloring. Submerge the eggshell in the liquid and leave it for 24 hours.
5. Remove the eggshell geode from the water. Lay it on a paper towel to dry. Your eggshell will be full of brightly colored crystals.

What's Happening?

On the outside, geodes look like regular rocks. When you break them open, you find sparkling crystals. Geodes are formed from decomposed fossils and bubbles trapped in molten rock. Water flows through the bubbles and leaves behind minerals that form crystals. Large geodes can take up to a million years to form.

Frost Crystals

You don't have to wait until winter for frost to grow on your window.

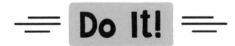

Supplies

Epsom salt, Water, Dish soap, Window, Bowl, Measuring cup, Mixing spoon, Paper towel

1. In a bowl, dissolve ½ cup of hot tap water and ⅓ cup Epsom salt. If the salt won't dissolve, heat the bowl in the microwave for 30 seconds and stir.
2. Mix two drops of dish soap to the salt solution.
3. Dip a paper towel into the mixture and wipe it onto a window. In about five minutes, you will see crystals form!

What's Happening?

Epsom salt is made up of tiny crystals. When you pour salt into water, it dissolves. When the water evaporates, the salt forms crystals again. The salt solution on the window creates a thin layer of crystals, much like frost on a window. Real frost is formed when a thin layer of moisture freezes and forms water crystals.

You might be wondering what the dish soap was for. Without the soap, the water and salt would form droplets on the window instead of spreading out. The soap makes the saltwater stick to the window instead of sticking to itself.

Rock Candy

Rock candy is crystals you can eat!

Do It!

Supplies
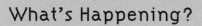

Sugar, Water, Measuring cup, Microwave-safe bowl, Tall jar, Skewer, Clothespin

1. Pour 1 cup of water and 3 cups of sugar into a microwave-safe bowl. Heat the bowl in the microwave for two minutes. Stir to dissolve the sugar. Pour the hot sugar solution into a jar and let it cool for 20 minutes.
2. Dip one end of a skewer in the sugar solution, and then dip it in dry sugar. Lay the skewer flat to cool.
3. Clip a clothespin to the non-sugared end of the skewer. Place the sugared end into the sugar solution. Balance the clip on the jar. The skewer should not touch the bottom of the jar.
4. Set the jar in a cool place and cover with a paper towel.
5. Check the candy every day for a week, or until the crystals are the size you want. Admire the crystals before you eat them!

What's Happening?

As the hot sugar solution cools, the sugar leaves the solution to form sugar crystals on the skewer. The sugar on the skewer act as seeds on which the sugar crystals start to grow.

Salt Crystals

Not all crystals are the same. Look carefully to see different shapes and patterns.

Do It!

Supplies

Table salt, Epsom salt, Salt substitute, 3 plastic cups, Water, Mixing spoon, Measuring cup, Refrigerator, Marker

1. Pour ½ cup of each salt into a cup and label them.
2. Pour ½ cup of hot tap water into each cup. Stir until the salt is dissolved. Place the cups in the refrigerator where they won't be disturbed.
3. After 24 hours, the cups should be full of crystals. If not, put them back in the refrigerator one more day. Pour out any remaining liquid.
4. Look closely at the crystals. What shape are they? How are they similar? Different?

What's Happening?

When salt dissolves in water, the charged ions that make up the salt molecules split up and float in the water. For example, table salt is sodium chloride, so there are sodium ions and chlorine ions. As the water evaporates, fewer ions fit in the water, so they pair up to make sodium chloride again. This creates crystals. The crystals grow as more molecules are added. Table salt and salt substitute make square crystals. Epsom salt makes spiky crystals.

Speleothems

You don't need to live in a cave to create stalactites and stalagmites.

Supplies

2 jars or cups, Wool or cotton yarn, Tray or cookie sheet, Small paper plate, Washing soda, Water, Mixing spoon, Measuring spoon

Do It!

1. Fill the jars with hot tap water and stir in several spoonfuls of washing soda. Keep adding washing soda until it will no longer dissolve in the water. Place the two jars on a tray with the small paper plate between them.

2. Cut three pieces of yarn about 24 inches long. Twist the yarn together and put one end in each jar. Make sure the ends are pushed down into the solution. The section between the jars should droop a little.

3. Leave the jars in a warm, dry place where they will not be disturbed. Depending on the temperature and humidity, it could take from one to four days for speleothems to form. After an hour or so, you should see the solution drip from the yarn onto the plate. Too much dripping will dissolve the stalagmites before they form. Too little dripping, and they won't grow at all. Slide the jars closer or farther apart to adjust the dripping. Soon, you will have your very own speleothems!

What's Happening?

Stalactites and stalagmites form when water seeps through rocks above caves. As the water moves through the rock, it dissolves small amounts of minerals. When the water drips from the cave ceiling, small amounts of the mineral are left behind, eventually leaving an icicle-like stalactite. The water that drips onto the cave floor also contains minerals that build up to form stalagmites. It can take hundreds of years to form speleothems.

In this experiment, the water and the minerals in the washing soda (sodium carbonate) traveled along the yarn instead of through rock. These speleothems, stalactites, and stalagmites form in a few days instead of a hundred years!

What If?

What if you dissolve a crystal-making substance other than washing soda? Try baking soda, Epsom salt, table salt, or sugar.

Gelatin Plastic

Gelatin plastic is used for everything from pill capsules to makeup. It's also found in some of your favorite sweets, such as marshmallows.

Supplies

Unflavored gelatin, Water, Bowl, Spoon, Measuring spoon, Jar lid, Food coloring

1. In a bowl, add 3 tablespoons of hot tap water, 2½ teaspoons of gelatin, and some drops of food coloring.
2. Mix the gelatin until it is dissolved. Before the gelatin cools, pour it into the jar lid. Use a spoon to push out any bubbles.
3. Leave the gelatin in a cool, dry spot for three to five days, until it is completely dry. Then remove it from the mold. How does the gelatin plastic feel? Can you bend it?

What's Happening?

All plastics are made of polymers, or chains of molecules. In gelatin plastic, that molecule is collagen. Collagen comes from the bones and skin of pigs and cows. When collagen is heated, it forms the chains that make plastic so strong and flexible.

Make a Bouncy Ball

Make your own bouncy ball at home with just a few household chemicals.

Supplies

Borax soap, Water, School glue, Cornstarch, Measuring spoon, Measuring cup, 2 cups, Mixing spoon, Fork, Food coloring

1. In one cup, mix ½ cup of hot tap water and 1 teaspoon of Borax. Stir until dissolved.
2. In another cup, mix 1 tablespoon of glue, one tablespoon of cornstarch, and two drops of food coloring.
3. Pour the glue mixture into the Borax. Let it sit for 15 seconds. Use a fork to pull the glue out.
4. Knead the glue into a ball. If it's sticky, put it in the Borax for a few more seconds.
5. Roll it into a ball and start bouncing! How high does it bounce? Does it bounce better on hard floors or carpet? When you are done, store your ball in a sealed bag.

What's Happening?

Glue contains long chains of a molecule called polyvinyl acetate, or PVA. PVA makes the glue sticky. The Borax links these chains together to make a strong, stretchy mesh. Cornstarch binds the mesh together so that it holds a round shape. The stretchy mesh is flexible, so when it hits the ground, it squishes a bit. However, the ball is elastic, so it returns to its round shape as it bounces back up. The result is a bouncy plastic ball!

Plastic Milk

ADULT NEEDED

Before plastic was made from petroleum, it was made from milk. In the early 1900s, milk was used to make buttons, beads, and jewelry. You can make your very own buttons and beads from milk, too!

Supplies

Whole milk; Vinegar; Measuring spoon; Measuring cup; Bowl; Spoon; Strainer; Paper towels; Food coloring, glitter, cookie cutters (optional)

═ Do It! ═

1. Have a grown-up help you heat 1 cup of milk on the stove until it is hot but not boiling. You will see steam rise off the milk when it is ready. Pour the hot milk into a bowl.

2. Add 4 teaspoons of vinegar and stir for about one minute. The milk will get chunky.

3. Pour the chunky milk through a strainer and wait until the chunks are cool enough to touch. Rinse off the milk chunks in the sink under running water and press them together. How does the milk plastic feel? How much plastic did you get from one cup of milk?

4. After the plastic is rinsed, wrap it in paper towels and squeeze out any extra water. Mold the plastic into any shape you like. You can add food coloring, glitter, or use a cookie cutter to make shapes. Use a toothpick to make holes to make beads for a necklace. Leave the milk plastic on paper towels to dry for at least two days.

What's Happening?

Plastics can look and feel very different, but the one thing they have in common are the molecules they are made of. All plastics are made of polymers, or chains of molecules. In milk plastic, that molecule is casein. In a glass of milk, casein is a monomer, or single molecule. When you add an acid like vinegar to the milk, the casein molecules bunch together and form chains of casein molecules that look like slimy, white chunks. These chunks are milk plastic. When it is dry, the plastic is hard, shiny, and durable.

What If?

What if you make milk plastic from cold milk instead of hot? What if you use skim milk or cream? What if you use more vinegar, or less vinegar, or even a different acid, such as lemon juice?

Pencils Through a Plastic Bag

Add drama to this experiment by holding the bag of water over someone's head!

Supplies

Resealable plastic sandwich bag, 3 or more sharpened pencils, Water

Do It!

1. Fill the plastic bag about ¾ full of water and seal it tightly.
2. Poke the pointy end of a pencil into the bag. Without hesitating, slide the pencil the rest of the way through so that the pointy end is on one side of the bag and the eraser is on the other. Does the water leak out? Can you add more pencils? How many pencils can you poke through the bag?

What's Happening?

Polymers are simply long chains of molecules that are connected. Many common materials are made of polymers: rubber balloons, nylon pantyhose, paper, and plastic bags. When the pencils are pushed into the plastic bag, they simply slide between the polymer chains. The polymer chains are held together around the hole created by the pencil, preventing the water from leaking out.

Shrinking Plastic

Use thermoplastics to make some incredible shrinking creations. **ADULT NEEDED**

Supplies

Clear plastic takeout tray (make sure it has a #6 recycle symbol), Permanent markers, Ruler, Scissors, Aluminum foil, Cookie sheet, Oven, Hole punch (optional)

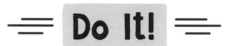
Do It!

1. Preheat the oven to 325°F.
2. Cut a flat piece of plastic into a 4" x 4" square. Cut other shapes too, and color them with a permanent marker. Use a hole punch to make a hole for jewelry.
3. Line the cookie sheet with foil. Lay the plastic on the sheet. Make sure they are not touching.
4. Place the sheet in the oven for three minutes. Let the plastic cool completely (about five minutes) before removing them.
5. Measure the square. How much did it shrink?

What's Happening?

The clear plastic in this experiment is made of tangled chains of polystyrene molecules, or polymers. To make the thin, clear plastic, the polystyrene is heated and rolled out so that the polymer chains straighten out. The plastic is cooled very quickly so that it holds its shape. Plastics made in this way are called thermoplastics. If you reheat a thermoplastic, the polymer chains will curl back up to their original shape, and the thin plastic shrinks!

A Quick Lesson on Slime

All slimes are non-Newtonian fluids, which is just a fancy way of saying that they don't act how most liquids are supposed to act. Isaac Newton came up with a way to describe how liquids flow called viscosity. Thin liquids, such as water, have a low viscosity. Thick liquids, such as molasses or ketchup, have a high viscosity. Viscosity is not the same as density. For example, vegetable oil is more viscous (flows slower) but is less dense than water. A liquid is non-Newtonian when its viscosity can be changed by other factors, such as stirring, stretching, or squeezing.

How Do You Make a Slime?

Slimes are made of polymers, or chains of molecules like a long chain of paper clips. Slime happens when you add a cross-linking chemical that connects those chains. (Think attaching strings to different paper clip chains, and then tangling them together so they can't easily come apart.) All the slime recipes here have two ingredients: a polymer and a cross linker.

Soap Slime

Here's a soft slime that smells good, too!

Supplies

Cornstarch, Shampoo, Spoon, Bowl

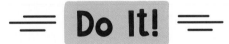 Do It!

1. Pour ¼ cup of cornstarch into the bowl, and then squirt a small amount of shampoo into the bowl. Mix them together.
2. Keep mixing in small amounts of shampoo until the mixture comes together. Take the slime out of the bowl and finish mixing it together with your hands. Add more cornstarch if the slime is too sticky or shampoo if it is too stiff.

What If?

What if you use other soaps like hand soap, body soap, or even shaving cream?

Oobleck

This slime is named after the ooey, gooey slime that falls from the sky in the Dr. Seuss book of the same name. It is simple, slimy fun, and the easiest slime to make.

Supplies

Cornstarch, Water, Measuring cup, Bowl, Spoon (optional), Food coloring (optional)

Do It!

1. Pour 1 cup of cornstarch into a bowl.
2. Add about ¼ cup of water and a few drops of food coloring. Use a spoon or your hands to mix the oobleck. If it is too dry, add more water. If it is too wet, add more cornstarch.
3. Put your finger on top of the oobleck and push down slowly. Then use your finger (or whole hand) to hit the oobleck hard. What happens?

What If?

What if you adjust the amount of water? What is the least amount of water needed to make oobleck? What is the most water you can add so that it still has slimy properties?

Snot

This slime bears a striking resemblance to the mucus that comes out of your nose!

Do It!

1. Pour ½ cup of glue (a 4-oz. bottle) and ½ cup of liquid starch into the bowl or bag.
2. If you use a bag, push the air out and seal the bag. Use your hands to squish the bag and mix the glue and starch. Once it's mixed, you can take it out and play with it over the bowl. Keep the bag for storage later.
3. If you use a bowl, use the spoon or your hands to mix the glue and starch. This is definitely the messier option, but that's the whole point of slime.
4. After the glue and starch are mixed, try rolling your slime into a ball and stretching it out. Grab a handful of slime, hold it high over the bowl, and let it flow from your hands. How long can the snotty slime flow before it breaks?

Supplies

Clear school glue, Liquid starch, Measuring cup, Bowl or quart-sized resealable freezer bag, Spoon

What If?

What if you add more glue than starch, or more starch than glue? Try to get the slime solid enough to roll it into a bouncing ball. How high can the ball bounce?

Sticky Slime

This is a classic slime recipe for the ooziest, stickiest, slimiest slime you can make. Add some food coloring to increase the slime factor even more!

Supplies

White school glue, Borax soap, Water, Measuring cup, Measuring spoon, 2 bowls, 2 mixing spoons, Food coloring (optional)

Do It!

1. In one bowl, add ½ cup of glue (a 4-oz. bottle) and ½ cup of water. Use a spoon to mix them together.
2. In another bowl, mix 1 cup of warm water with 1 teaspoon of Borax soap. Make sure the soap is completely dissolved.
3. Add the soap mixture to the glue mixture, and mix slowly with a spoon. Once the slime thickens, use your hands to knead it together until it is completely mixed. Now your slime is ready for sticky stretching and squishing!

What If?

What if you add more Borax to the soap solution? What if you add less? How does the amount of soap affect the stickiness or ooziness of your slime?

Edible Slime

ADULT NEEDED

Yes, you can eat this version of slime, but it is probably more fun to play with than to eat.

Supplies

Soluble fiber that contains psyllium, such as Metamucil; Water; Glass microwave-safe bowl; Measuring cup; Spoon

Do It!

1. Pour 1 cup of water and 1 teaspoon of soluble fiber into a bowl. Stir well until the fiber is completely dissolved.
2. Heat the bowl in the microwave for four minutes. Stop heating as soon as you see the mixture boil.
3. Stir the mixture, and then microwave for another two minutes. Repeat this process four more times. Let the slime cool completely before playing with it.

What If?

What happens if you use more soluble fiber in the slime? How about less? What if you continue to heat the slime more than four times? What if you only heat the slime two times instead of four?

Magnetic Slime

Adding iron to the slime gives it surprising magnetic properties.

Supplies

Ingredients for Snot or Sticky Slime, ¼ cup iron oxide powder, Strong magnet, Styrofoam plate

Do It!

1. Make Snot or Sticky Slime, except add ¼ cup of iron oxide powder to the soap or liquid starch before adding the glue.

2. Make a small ball of slime and put it on a Styrofoam plate. Put the magnet under the plate and drag it around under the slime. Can you move it with the magnet? Put all the slime on the plate and spread it out. What happens if you move the magnet underneath the plate now?

What If?

What if you try magnetizing different types of slime? Which one responds to the magnet the most?

Glow-in-the-Dark Slime

Create spooky slime with some glow-in-the-dark science.

Supplies

Ingredients for Oobleck, Sticky, or Edible Slime; Tonic water; Green food coloring (optional); Black light

Do It!

1. Make Oobleck, Sticky, or Edible Slime, but with tonic water instead of regular water.

2. Place the slime under a black light to see it glow. The tonic water will glow blue, but you can add green food coloring to give it a more traditional slimy color.

Making Prints

How can you tell who has been at the scene of the crime? Fingerprints, of course!

Supplies

Inkpad, White or light-colored balloon

1. Roll your thumb on the inkpad so that the pad of your thumb is covered with ink.
2. Flatten the balloon. Carefully roll your thumb across the balloon to make a clean fingerprint.
3. Blow up the balloon and tie it off. Your fingerprint should be enlarged so that you can clearly see the details. Be careful not to touch or smudge your fingerprint until it is dry.
4. Inspect your fingerprint. What patterns and shapes do you see?

What's Happening?

Blowing up the balloon stretches the ink fingerprint so that you can inspect its details. You should see one or more of the main fingerprint patterns: whorl, loop, and arch. You might also see some of the tiny details that let crime solvers tell one fingerprint from another. For example, a delta is where three lines or valleys come together and bifurcation is where a line or ridge splits in two. The tiny white dots are sweat pores.

Dusting for Prints

Need to remove fingerprints from a crime scene? Just dust for prints using a fine powder.

Supplies

Soft makeup brush (new works best); Cocoa powder; White paper; Scotch tape; Smooth, hard objects (a mug or tabletop) to collect prints

1. Rub your index finger across your forehead, through your hair, or down the side of your nose to collect as much oil as you can onto your finger.
2. Press your finger firmly on a mug, table, or another smooth, hard surface.
3. Dip the brush into the powder so it is coated all over.
4. Gently brush back and forth across the print so the powder sticks to the fingerprint.
5. Sweep away any extra powder.
6. Carefully and firmly lay a piece of tape down over the fingerprint so there are no bubbles.
7. Pull up the tape and stick it onto the white paper. Are you able to clearly see the fingerprint?

What's Happening?

The fingerprint you left on the mug, like any fingerprint at a crime scene, is made of the oil, sweat, and dust on your finger. Greasy fingers leave the best prints. The cocoa powder sticks to the oil and grease, which then sticks to the tape, so you are able to transfer the fingerprint on to the paper.

Lifting Prints

This chemical reaction solidifies your fingerprints permanently.

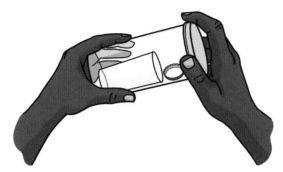

Supplies

Clean wide-mouth jar with a lid (pasta sauce or pickle jars work well); Bottle cap; Super glue; Small, smooth, hard item to collect prints (such as a bottle cap or playing card)

═ Do It! ═

1. Rub your index finger across your forehead, through your hair, or down the side of your nose to collect as much oil as you can onto your finger.

2. Press your finger firmly on the object you are using to collect prints. You can also make a fingerprint on the inside of the glass jar.

3. Lay the jar on its side and gently place the object in the jar. Make sure each print is facing up and is not covered.

4. Carefully add just enough glue into the bottle cap to cover the bottom of the cap.

5. Place the bottle cap into the jar with the objects and put the lid tightly on the jar.

6. Let the jar sit for one hour under a lamp or in some other warm place. If you don't want to wait, you can heat the jar with a hair dryer on high for ten minutes.

7. Take the jar outside and remove the lid so the glue fumes can escape. Be careful not to tip the jar so the objects and bottle cap of glue don't fall on each other.

8. Remove each of the objects and inspect the fingerprints. Don't forget the fingerprint you left inside the jar!

What's Happening?

This method of collecting fingerprints is called *cyanoacrylate fuming,* after the chemical found in super glue. When the cyanoacrylate heats up, it evaporates into the air inside the jar. When the chemical comes in contact with the sweat and oil in the fingerprint, it reacts to form a hard, white substance that you can see. This method was first used in Japan in 1978 and is now used widely around the world because it's cheap, easy, and reliable—and not as messy as dusting!

What If?

What if you try this same method on other materials? Try plastic, wood, metal, Styrofoam, and cloth and see which material works best.

Hot Invisible Ink

Every secret agent needs a way to send messages that won't be discovered by the enemy! This ink needs a heat source to be revealed.

ADULT NEEDED

Supplies

Vinegar, Paper, Cotton swabs, Heat source (lamp, oven, iron, or hair dryer)

Do It!

1. Dip a cotton swab into the vinegar and write a message on a clean piece of paper. Let the paper dry completely.

2. Heat up your paper to reveal the message. Choose one of these methods:
   - Hold the paper close to, but not touching, a lamp until the message appears.
   - With an adult's help, heat the oven to 300°F. Put the paper on a cookie sheet and bake for 10 minutes.
   - With an adult's help, heat the iron on the "Cotton" setting, and iron your paper until the message appears.
   - Set a hair dryer on high and move it back and forth a couple of inches from the paper until the message appears.

What's Happening?

Vinegar is a mild acid and weakens the paper wherever you wrote your message. The acid also stays on the paper after the invisible ink has dried. When you heat the paper, the acidic message burns or turns brown before the rest of the paper.

What If?

What if you use milk, sugar water, lemon juice, or any other fruit drinks instead of vinegar?

Acid Ink

It takes a chemical reaction to create this secret ink!

Supplies

Paper, Baking soda, Water, Small bowl, Measuring spoon, Cotton swabs, Grape juice

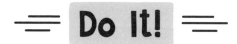

Do It!

1. Mix 2 tablespoons of baking soda with 2 tablespoons of water in the small bowl.
2. Dip a cotton swab into the baking soda mixture and write your message on a clean piece of paper. Let the paper dry completely.
3. Use another cotton swab to paint grape juice over the paper and reveal the message.

What's Happening?

The baking soda, a base, reacts with the grape juice, an acid, to produce a different color on the paper.

Milky Ink

Be sure to come up with a mooo-ving secret message for this milky ink!

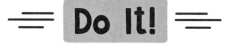

Do It!

Supplies

Paper, Whole milk, Cotton swab, 2 sharpened pencils

1. Dip a cotton swab into the milk and write a message on a clean piece of paper. Let it dry.
2. Take two sharpened pencils, and rub the graphite (the black parts that write) together so that graphite dust falls on the paper.
3. Use your finger to gently rub the graphite into the paper and reveal the message.

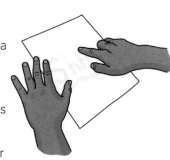

What's Happening?

It is very important to use whole milk for this experiment, because whole milk has a lot of fat. When your message dries on the paper, most of the milk evaporates but the fat stays on the paper. Graphite sticks to the fat more than the paper, allowing your invisible message to be revealed.

What If?

What if you use a different kind of milk with less fat, such as 1% or 2%?

Wax Resist Ink

This simple method of messaging will result in a colorful message!

Supplies

**White crayon, Paper,
Watercolor paints,
Paintbrush, Water**

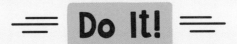

Do It!

1. Write a message on the paper with the white crayon.
2. Use the paintbrush, water, and watercolors to paint all over the paper. Darker colors, such as blue, green, and red, are best.

What's Happening?

Wax repels water! In this experiment, the watercolor paints will not stick to the white crayon message, so your message is revealed.

What If?

What if you try sending a message on wax paper or other kinds of paper?

Glowing Ink

You can only see messages written in this ink with a black light. How revealing!

Supplies

**Paper, Clear or
white liquid laundry
detergent, Cotton
swab, Black light**

Do It!

1. Dip a cotton swab into the detergent and write your message on a clean piece of paper. Let it dry.
2. To reveal the message, simply dim or turn off the lights and shine the black light onto the paper.

What's Happening?

Laundry detergent contains a type of chemical called "phosphors." Phosphors fluoresce or glow in the ultraviolet light given off by the sun (and black lights) and make your clothes look bright. To see the phosphors in your clothes, go into a dark room and shine the black light. The phosphors in your secret message also fluoresce when the black light shines on your paper.

What If?

What if you write a message with other fluorescent materials, such as petroleum jelly or tonic water?

Triple Pen Inspection

Chromatography is a scientific way of figuring out if two writing samples came from the same pen. This is a very handy tool for secret-agent scientists!

Supplies

Paper coffee filter, Scissors, 4 pencils, 4 large clear glasses, Ruler, 3 ballpoint pens that have the same color ink but different brands, Rubbing alcohol, Vinegar, Ammonia, Water, Ultraviolet lamp (optional)

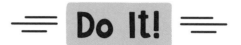 **Do It!**

1. Cut the coffee filter into four strips at least 2 inches wide.
2. Wrap one end of each of the coffee filter strips around a pencil.
3. Tape it in place so when the pencil rests across the top of the glass, the strip hangs into the glass without touching the sides and just barely touching the bottom.
4. Use a pencil to draw a line across the strip, exactly ½ inch from the bottom.
5. With each of the pens, make a pea-sized dot, ½ inch away from the line you drew on the bottom of the strip.
6. Use the pencil to label which dot came from each pen below each dot.
7. At the top of the strip, label which liquid the strip will be placed into (alcohol, vinegar, ammonia, or water).
8. Remove the filter strips from the glasses.

9. Pour a small amount of each liquid into a glass, just filling the bottom.

10. Replace the pencils across the top of the glasses so that the bottom of the filter strip touches the liquid, but the ink dot does not. You may need to adjust the amount of liquid in the glass. (Take the filter strip out of the glass before you do this; if you splash liquid directly on the ink, you'll have to redo the experiment!)

11. Wait until the liquid spreads up the filter through the ink dot and reaches the pencil.

12. Take the strips off the pencils and lay them flat to dry.

Once they're dry, inspect the strips carefully. You'll see spots or smears of color between the original ink mark. These spots or smears are the ingredients of the ink. If the spots are not obvious, try holding the paper under an ultraviolet lamp (black light). Some compounds can be seen better this way.

How many different spots did each of the inks produce? How many different colors do you see?

What's Happening?

Scientists use chromatography to figure out the ingredients in mixtures such as ink. When the mixture or ink is dissolved in a solvent, it separates into its different ingredients.

In this experiment, we used four solvents: water, ammonia, alcohol, and vinegar. As the solvent moves up the coffee filter, it separates out the ingredients.

Similar ingredients will travel up the paper the same distance, so scientists are able to identify exactly what the ingredients are. The pattern that is created is like a fingerprint for identifying the ink.

Compare the dots for the different pens. Do any have dots or smears of color at the same distance? If so, this means the inks in those pens have similar ingredients.

What If?

What if you try analyzing other mixtures with chromatography, such as lipstick, markers, or other types or colors of pens?

Liquid Magnifier

Magnifying glasses come in handy for all sorts of secret agent investigations. But what can you do when you don't have one? Make your own, of course!

Supplies

Clear 2-liter soda bottle, Marker, Scissors, Water

Do It!

1. Draw a circle about 3 inches in diameter on the soda bottle, near the top where the bottle curves the most.
2. Use the scissors to cut out the circle. It should be curved, like a small bowl.
3. Pour water into the bowl so that it's about half full.
4. Hold the magnifying bowl over whatever you need to enlarge.

What's Happening?

Magnifying lenses are convex or thicker in the middle. This shape bends the light rays so that objects close to the lens appear larger. The water in your curved soda bottle bowl is also thicker in the middle and bends light in the same way, making a liquid magnifying glass!

Straw Magnifier

This little magnifier is easy to carry and even hide in the palm of your hand. Just add a couple drops of water and anything tiny will become large!

Do It!

Supplies

Straw, Scissors, Ruler, Clear packing tape, Water

1. Cut off a piece of straw about ¼ inch long.
2. Cover one end of the straw piece with a small piece of packing tape.
3. Fill the straw to the top with water, so that a big drop sits above the level of the straw.
4. Hold your straw magnifier over something tiny and look into the straw to see it get instantly bigger!

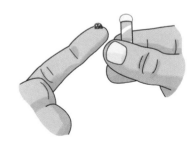

What's Happening?

Water is sticky, especially on top of a cup (or straw) full of water where it meets the air. Scientists call this *surface tension*. The water on top of the straw bulges up because the sticky surface tension is holding the water together. This shape bends the light rays, so objects under the straw appear larger.

Build a Periscope

With a periscope, a secret agent can see over walls and around corners without being seen!

Supplies

Clean quart-sized milk or juice carton, Scissors, 2 mirrors about 2½" x 3½" in size, Tape

═ Do It! ═

1. Cut the top off of the carton.
2. Cut a small square about ¼ inch from the bottom of the carton for the eyehole.
3. Cut a large square, about twice the size of your eyehole, ¼ inch from the top of the carton on the opposite side from the eyehole. This will be the view hole where light comes into the front of the periscope.
4. Tape the short end of a mirror to the bottom of the eyehole so that it's facing up.

5. Tape the other end of the mirror to the front of the periscope. When you look through the eyehole, you should be able to see straight up to the ceiling.
6. Tape the short end of the other mirror to the very top of the carton, above the view hole, so that it's facing down.
7. Tape the bottom of the mirror to the back of the carton.

When you look through the eyehole, you should be able to see straight through the view hole! Use your periscope to look over a table and around a corner.

What's Happening?

You see things when light bounces or reflects off an object to your eye. The mirrors in the periscope reflect the light that comes in from the view hole. The top mirror reflects the light down to the bottom mirror, and the bottom mirror reflects the light into your eye.

When you look through the eyehole, it seems like you're seeing something directly in front of you, at eye level. But you're actually seeing something much higher!

To test this out, while looking through the periscope, put your hand on the carton where you think the view hole is. Did you find it right away? It's harder than you think!

What If?

What if you have a longer periscope? How will the image you see change? Try taping two cartons together to make a super long periscope.

Camera Obscura: Pinhole

Before modern photography, artists experimented with projecting images on a screen. In Latin, *camera obscura* means "dark chamber." The camera obscura you will make is portable, but the earliest examples were rooms that were blacked out entirely, or chambers with a tiny hole through which an image of the outside world was projected on the walls.

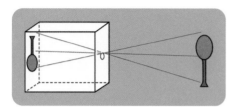

Supplies

Empty cereal box (including the bag inside), Ruler, Marker, Scissors, Duct tape (or black electrical tape), Safety pin or thumbtack, Dark room with a small lamp, Aluminum foil (optional)

Do It!

1. Fold the box so it's flat. Measure 2 inches from the bottom with the ruler and mark a straight line across the bottom. Cut the bottom off the box using the guideline. Then, refold the boxes so they are box-shaped again. Tape up the bottom of the short box so that no light can get through.

2. Cut the cereal bag in half and use one piece to cover the top of the short box. Stretch the bag tightly over the box and use duct tape secure it.

3. Put the tall box back on top of the short box and tape them back together. Be careful to cover the seam with tape so no light can get in. If you want to be extra careful, cover the whole box with aluminum foil.

4. Use the safety pin or thumbtack to make a tiny hole in the center of the bottom of the box.

5. Turn off all lights in the room except for the small lamp and put the open end of the cereal box on your face. Point the pinhole at the lamp. What do you see?

What's Happening?

When you look into your camera obscura box, you should see an upside image of the lamp projected on the screen. Because light has to travel through a straight line and through the tiny pinhole, the image you see is flipped in both directions, as shown above.

What If?

Try changing the size of your pinhole. What happens to the size of the image if you use a larger hole? How about the sharpness of the image?

Adjust the distance between the pinhole and the screen. What happens to the size and sharpness of the image when your screen is closer or farther from the pinhole? You could use a smaller box inside of a large box to have an adjustable screen.

Camera Obscura: Lens

A more advanced camera obscura uses a lens instead of a pinhole. This means you can use your viewer outside in the daylight, but now you'll need to focus your camera to see the image clearly.

Supplies

Large shoebox, Cereal box (or other source of thin cardboard), Scissors, Marker or pen, Aluminum foil, Wax paper, Magnifying glass or lens from reading glasses (you can find these at drug stores or dollar stores), Duct tape (or black electrical tape)

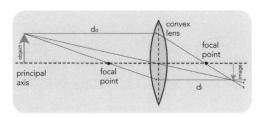

═ Do It! ═

1. Cut a round hole on the short end of the shoebox, slightly smaller than your lens or magnifying glass. Tape the lens to the outside of your box over the hole.

2. Cut a rectangular hole on the opposite end of the shoebox that is large enough to look through with both of your eyes.

3. Cut a rectangle from the extra cardboard that fits exactly inside the box. Cut out the center of this rectangle, leaving a 1-inch border. Cover the hole with a piece of wax paper and tape it into place so that it is stretched tight. This will be the screen for your image.

4. Place the screen inside the box between the eyeholes and the lens. Point the lens end of the box at a window or other bright light. Slide the screen back and forth until you see a bright, focused image. Tape the screen in place.

5. Put the cover on your shoebox and tape it in place so no extra light gets in. Look through the eyeholes at the window. What do you see? How does the image compare to the pinhole camera obscura?

6. Take your camera obscura outside and look around. You can even use duct tape to attach the box to the bill of a baseball hat so that it's wearable!

What's Happening?

A camera obscura with a lens is one step closer to our modern cameras. The lens allows you to have a larger hole, which lets more light through and creates images that are bigger and brighter.

With a lens, light is no longer simply traveling in a straight line to create an image (as in the pinhole camera obscura). Instead, the light bends as it travels through the glass to a focal point that depends on the shape and size of the glass lens. Magnifying glasses (and reading glasses) are thicker in the middle. This type of lens is called a convex lens and produces images that can be projected on a screen, unlike a concave lens that is thinner in the middle.

Colorful Cones

Use a little chemistry to create a crazily colorful campfire!

ADULT NEEDED

Supplies

Pinecones (4 or more), Bucket or large bowl, Measuring cup, Large spoon, Paper towels, Coloring chemicals (at least one of these, but you can use some or all)

- Table salt (sodium chloride)
- Borax (sodium borate)
- Plaster of Paris (calcium sulfate)
- Epsom salt (magnesium sulfate)
- Salt substitute* (potassium chloride)
- Pool algaecide* (copper sulfate)
- De-icer* (calcium chloride)

*Check the labels to make sure that the product you have includes the chemical listed here.

Do It!

1. Pour 8 cups of hot tap water into the bucket or bowl. With an adult's help, add 1 cup of just one of the coloring chemicals to the water and mix it in with the large spoon until the chemical is completely dissolved. Only use one chemical at a time.

2. Put four pinecones in the bucket and let them soak for eight hours or overnight.

3. Take out the pinecones and put them on a paper towel to dry. It may take a couple of days for them to dry completely.

4. Make as many pinecones as you like with the other coloring chemicals on the list. Just do a separate batch for each chemical.

5. The next time your family lights up the fireplace, or has a campfire or barbecue, have an adult add the pinecones and observe the colors of the flames. (But don't put the pinecones in the fire while you're cooking food.)

What's Happening?

The chemicals create different colors when they burn because of their atoms. All atoms have a nucleus, made of protons and electrons, around which electrons spin and move very fast. The electrons in different atoms have different (but very specific) energy levels that scientists like to describe as steps on a staircase. When an electron gains energy from heat or light (like when you burn chemicals), it gains energy and jumps up to a higher step. Eventually the electrons will fall back down to their original energy level and give up that extra energy in the form of light. The color of the light depends on how far down the staircase it had to jump. Red, orange, and yellow light have less energy and correspond to smaller steps than green, blue, and violet. The size of the steps and the color of the light given off depend on the type of atom. In this experiment, chemicals with copper give off a green or blue light, while those with calcium give off an orange light.

What If?

What if you try to identify which chemical was used on a pinecone just by looking at its flame?

What if you add more than one of the chemicals to the pinecone at a time? (The chemicals we use here are all salts and will not react with each other.)

Glow Sticks

Glow sticks use chemicals to produce light in all sorts of different colors. Can you make your glow stick glow all night long?

Supplies

A dark room, 3 glow sticks (all the same color), 2 tall cups, Hot (but not boiling) water, Ice water, Thermometer, Clock

Do It!

1. Label the cups "hot" and "cold." Pour hot water and ice water into the appropriate cups. Make sure the water is deep enough to cover most of the glow stick.
2. Check the temperature of the cups and the room. The temperatures should be at least 20°F apart. Add ice or hot water to the cups if they aren't.
3. Following the directions on the glow stick package, activate each glow stick. Then place a glow stick in each cup of water and stir. After one minute of stirring, turn out the lights and compare their brightness.
4. Place the "ice" cup in the freezer, and put the "hot" cup in a warm place. Leave the other glow stick on the counter at room temperature. Which glow stick glowed the longest? Did the temperature affect the brightness?

What's Happening?

Glow stick insides are made of hydrogen peroxide and a tiny glass bottle of phenyl oxalate ester plus a fluorescent dye. When you break the glass bottle inside the tube, the two chemicals mix, which releases light. This is called chemiluminescence. Heat adds extra energy to the glow stick and speeds up the reaction, causing the stick to glow brighter, but for a shorter time. Cooling the glow stick slows down the reaction and the light is dimmer but lasts much longer.

Glowing Groceries

Did you know you probably have glow-in-the-dark food in your pantry right now? **ADULT NEEDED**

Do It!

Supplies

Dark closet, 2 clear plastic cups, Tonic water, Bleach, Black light (found at party stores), Dropper

1. Pour some tonic water into both cups. Turn off the lights in your closet and turn on the black light. What happens to the tonic water under the black light?
2. Have an adult fill the dropper with the bleach. Warning: Be extra careful with bleach as it can stain anything it touches.
3. Add a drop or two of bleach into one cup of tonic water while it is still under the black light. What do you see? If nothing changes, add a few more drops. Also, do not drink the tonic water with bleach. Pour it down the drain when you are done.

What's Happening?

Tonic water gets its distinctive bitter taste from quinine, which absorbs light energy and re-emits it as lower-energy, blue, visible light. When you add bleach, it reacts with the quinine to break some of its chemical bonds so that it is no longer able to absorb the ultraviolet light.

Candy Crunch

Have you heard this urban myth? Well it's true! Biting wintergreen hard candies WILL make a spark!

 **Do It!**

Supplies

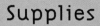

A completely dark closet, Mirror, 2 wintergreen flavored hard candies

1. To make a closet completely dark, place a towel at the bottom of the door.
2. Go into the dark closet with the mirror and one of the hard candies. Wait about two minutes for your eyes to adjust to the darkness.
3. Facing the mirror, put the candy in your mouth and chomp down on the candy with your teeth while your mouth is open. Did you see a blue-green spark of light?
4. If you have braces or aren't able to chomp the candy with your teeth, put the candies in a plastic bag and use pliers to break them up instead.

What's Happening?

The flavoring used in wintergreen candies is wintergreen oil, a fluorescent chemical that absorbs light at a shorter wavelength and releases it at a longer wavelength. When you bite the candy, you create a small electrical charge that reacts with the sugar to cause a spark of ultraviolet light. That ultraviolet light is absorbed by the wintergreen oil, and another flash of light is created.

Tape Tear

Duct tape can fix anything, right? It turns out you can do some enlightening science with it too!

Do It!

Supplies

A completely dark closet, Duct tape, Masking tape, Electrical tape, Scotch tape, Scissors

1. Cut two 18-inch pieces of duct tape. Fold over 1 inch on one end of each piece. These will be handles. Match up the folded ends and stick the tape together, sticky side to sticky side.
2. Take the tape into the dark closet. Wait about two minutes for your eyes to adjust to the darkness.
3. Hold the folded handle ends and pull the stuck tape apart. Look where the two pieces of tape met. You might see a faint glow of light. Try the same thing with the other tapes. Which tapes produced a glow? What color was the glow?

What's Happening?

As you pulled apart the tapes, you may have observed triboluminescence. In this case, when the tapes are stuck together, the sticky parts make weak chemical bonds. When you pull them apart, energy is released in the form of light.

Carnival Bottles

Ever try to win a stuffed animal by knocking over all the bottles in a carnival game? It's a lot easier if you stack the odds - and the bottles - in your favor.

Supplies

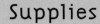

3 water bottles, Tennis balls, Measuring tape, Water, Table, Masking tape or chalk

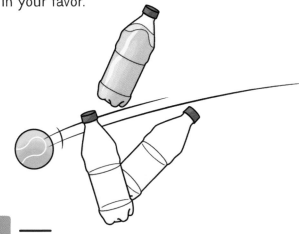

═ Do It! ═

1. Set up the table outdoors or somewhere you can throw balls without getting in trouble.

2. Fill all three bottles with water and set them on the table in a pyramid with two bottles on the bottom and one on top. Measure a distance 6 feet from the bottles and mark it with masking tape or chalk. This is where you will stand to throw balls at the bottles.

3. Throw a tennis ball at the bottles at least 12 times. Keep track of how many times you knock over one bottle, two bottles, and all three bottles.

4. Repeat the experiment with an empty bottle on top and two full bottles on the bottom, and again with a full bottle on top and two empty bottles on the bottom. In which setup were you able to knock over all the bottles the most? How about just one or two bottles?

What's Happening?

The key to this trick is center of gravity. Center of gravity is the balance point, or where the mass of an object is centered. To knock over all the bottles, the ball needs to hit at the center of gravity or lower.

When all three bottles are full of water, the center of gravity is somewhere near the top of the bottom bottles — almost in the center of the pyramid.

When only the top bottle has water, the center of gravity is in the middle of the top bottle. So, if you hit the bottom bottles, or the bottom of the top bottle, all the bottles will fall over. However, when the top bottle is empty and the bottom bottles are full, you need to hit the bottom half of the bottom bottles to knock over all three bottles, and that is very hard to do.

Arrow Switcheroo

The arrow points one way, and then the other. Which way do you go?

Supplies

Index card, Marker, Clear glass, Water

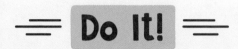
Do It!

1. Draw an arrow on the index card with a marker. Hold the arrow behind the empty glass. Which way does it point?
2. Fill the glass with water. Again, hold the arrow behind the glass. Which way does it point now?

What's Happening?

Light bends when it travels from one substance, such as air, into another, such as glass or water. Scientists call the bending of light "refraction." Light from the arrow bends when it hits the glass of water, and then again when it comes back out into the air before it hits your eyeball. The curved glass also acts as a lens, bending the light even more. The light bends so much that the arrow appears to change direction completely.

Bed of Tacks

This bed is too small for you, but it's just right for tired balloons.

Supplies

Cereal box, 226 flat-head tacks, 2 balloons, Ruler, Pencil, Scissors

Do It!

1. Cut an 8-inch square from the cereal box. Create a grid with the ruler by drawing a line every ½ inch from top to bottom, and again from side to side.
2. Push 225 tacks straight through the square where the lines intersect. Turn the board over with the pointy sides of the tacks facing up.
3. Blow up both balloons and tie them. Place the extra tack on the table, pointy side up. Press a balloon on top of it and push down. What happens? Push the other balloon on top of the bed of tacks. What happens to this balloon? Can you push hard enough to pop the balloon?

What's Happening?

When you push a balloon onto one tack, it pops because all the force is on that one point. With many tacks, that force is spread out, and there isn't enough force to pop the balloon. Force spread out over an area is called pressure. When a large force has a small area, the pressure is high, like the balloon pushed on one tack. When that same force is spread over a large area, the pressure is lower. That's why magicians can lie on a bed of nails. Standing on one nail would make a hole in your foot, but lying down on nails is quite comfortable!

Card Drop

Dropping a card is not as simple as it looks!

Supplies

Deck of cards, Audience

1. Pull two cards from the deck. Hold one flat (parallel to the ground) and the other straight up (perpendicular to the ground) at same height.
2. Ask your audience which card they think will hit the ground first, and then drop the cards. Which card hit the ground first?

What's Happening?

As the flat card falls, it stays flat as gravity pulls it down. If the card starts to tilt one way or the other, it creates lift that brings the card flat again. Because you cannot hold the card straight up, and the air in the room probably is not perfectly still, the perpendicular card will spin as you drop it. The spinning motion produces lift, which causes the card to glide sideways. The gliding means this card takes a couple seconds longer to reach the ground.

Diaper Deception

Actually, there is no real deception here – just science!

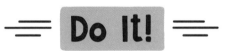 Do It!

Supplies

Diaper, Scissors, Large resealable plastic bag, Measuring cup, 3 cups that you cannot see through

1. To prepare, cut open the diaper and seal it inside the bag. Shake it until you see powder come out. When you see about a tablespoon of powder, take out the diaper and pour the powder into a cup.
2. In front of your audience, pour ¼ cup of water into one of the empty cups. Tell the audience to follow the cup with the water as you move the cups around.
3. Pour the water into the other empty cup and move the cups around again.
4. Finally, pour the water into the cup with the white powder. Move the cups around again, but make sure the cup with the water and powder is on your right. Ask the audience which cup has the water. Start on your left and turn each cup over. No water will pour out of any of the cups!

What's Happening?

Diapers are absorbent because of a powder called sodium polyacrylate. Water sticks to this long molecule, which grows longer to hold more water until it is saturated. Scientists call materials that absorb water "hygroscopic." Sodium polyacrylate can hold many times its weight in water, which is why nothing comes out of the cup!

Mind Control Motion

Move objects with only your mind – and a little help from a few electrons.

Supplies

Plastic bottle cap, Straw, Balloon, Empty soda can, Head of hair or wool sweater

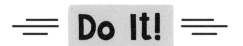

Do It!

Can Control

1. Lay the can on a flat surface on its side so that it's able to roll easily.

2. Blow up the balloon and tie it off. Rub the balloon on your hair or a wool sweater. Bring the balloon near the can and move it slowly away from the can. Does the can move? Make sure the can does not touch the balloon. Move the balloon to the other side of the can. Does its motion change?

Spinning Straw

1. Rub the straw on your hair or the wool sweater. Lay the straw across the top of the bottle cap so that it balances in the middle.

2. Slowly move your finger toward one end of the straw. Does the straw move? What happens if you move your finger toward other parts of the straw?

What's Happening?

Rubbing a straw or balloon on your hair (or a wool sweater) removes electrons from the hair and wool and puts them on the straw and balloon so that they are negatively charged. Opposite charges attract and like charges repel. When you bring the charged balloon near the soda can, the negative electrons on the balloon repel the negative electrons in the can. Some of those electrons move to the other side of the can. This makes the side of the can next to the balloon slightly positive so that it is attracted to the balloon and rolls toward it.

The same thing happens with the straw on the bottle cap. Here, the straw has extra electrons and repels the electrons in your finger. Your finger becomes just the tiniest bit positive, which is enough to attract the end of the straw and make it spin around the bottle cap.

Dollar Bill Drop

Offer a dollar bill to your volunteer, on the condition that they can catch it.

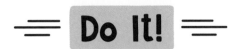

Do It!

Supplies

Dollar bill, Volunteer, Table

1. Have your volunteer rest their arm on the table with their hand hanging over the edge. Have them stick out their middle and index fingers. Hold the dollar bill long ways so that the very bottom of the bill is just between their fingers.
2. Tell the volunteer that you will drop the dollar bill and if they can catch it between their two fingers, they can keep it. Without warning your volunteer, drop the bill. Do they catch it? If not, try again.

What's Happening?

The human reaction time is about 0.2 seconds. This is the amount of time it takes your eyes to send a signal through your brain to your fingers to grab the bill. However, a dollar bill is about 6 inches long and it takes 0.18 seconds for gravity to pull the bill down 6 inches and out of your volunteer's reach. Very few people will be able to catch the dollar bill. By using the middle and index fingers, you guarantee they cannot because these are the slowest-moving fingers.

Now do the same experiment, except this time use a ruler to measure the reaction time. Use the distance in centimeters (d) that the ruler falls before you catch it to calculate your reaction time (t) using this equation: $t = (\sqrt{d})/22.1$

Toothpick Star

This trick is fun to do at the dinner table because all you need are toothpicks and water.

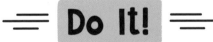

Do It!

Supplies

Toothpicks, Plate, Water

1. Bend five wooden toothpicks in half so that they snap but do not come apart completely. Arrange them on a plate, as shown.
2. Pour a spoonful of water in the very center and watch as the toothpicks move. What shape do they make now?

What's Happening?

Wood is made of fibers that are good at absorbing water. When you add water to the center of the toothpicks where they are broken, the fibers in the wood absorb the water and expand. The expanding wood pushes the toothpicks back to a straight shape until they bump into each other to make the star shape.

Tablecloth Tug

Add some drama to dinner by yanking the tablecloth out from under the dishes.

═ Do It! ═

1. Lay the tablecloth on the table so that there is just enough room for one place setting and at least several inches hang down over the front edge of the table. Make sure the tablecloth is completely smooth with no wrinkles or bumps.

2. Start with just the plate in the center of the tablecloth. You might also want to place a rug under the table just in case the plate falls on your first try.

3. The secret to this trick is confidence. Do not hesitate or all will be lost. With both hands, grab the part of the tablecloth that hangs down in front. Firmly and quickly yank the tablecloth straight down until it is all the way off the table. What happens to the plate?

4. Practice a few times with just the plate, and then add the silverware and empty glass. When you feel confident enough, pour some water in the glass.

What's Happening?

Isaac Newton's first law of motion is just as much about motion as it is about staying put. He said that an object will stay right where it is unless a force acts on it. Scientists call this tendency to stay put "inertia." If you apply the force to the tablecloth and not to the dishes, they will stay right where they are.

Heavier or more massive objects have more inertia. You may have noticed that the lighter objects with less inertia, such as the silverware, move a little bit while the heavier plate and glass stay put. That's because there is a very small force acting on the dishes: friction. Friction affects the motion of two things that are sliding against each other, like the silverware and tablecloth. You can reduce the friction by using a tablecloth that is very smooth.

Invisible Extinguisher

ADULT NEEDED

Why blow out a candle when you can use "magic"?

Supplies

Tall glass, Baking soda, Vinegar, Spoon, Votive candle, Lighter or matches

Do It!

1. Add two spoonfuls of baking soda to the glass. Pour in enough vinegar to more than cover the baking soda. While you wait for the bubbles in the glass to die down, light the candle.

2. After the bubbles stop, gently pour the gas that is in the glass (NOT the actual baking soda and vinegar) over the candle. What happens to the candle flame?

What's Happening?

Mixing baking soda and vinegar creates a chemical reaction that produces a large amount of carbon dioxide gas. This gas is heavier than air, so it stays in the bottom of the glass. The burning candle needs oxygen from the air to stay lit. The candle flame comes from a chemical reaction called combustion between the wax and oxygen in the air. When you pour the carbon dioxide from the glass onto the candle, oxygen cannot reach the flame and the candle goes out.

Marble Pick-up

Defy gravity by lifting a marble in a cup with no bottom!

Do It!

Supplies

Paper cup, Marble, Scissors

1. Cut the bottom out of the paper cup. Make sure the edges are smooth.

2. Place the marble on a smooth surface, such as a tabletop, and place the cup on top of the marble.

3. Place your hand over the cup and hold it by the edges. Use your wrist to move the cup in a circular motion on the table so that the marble rolls along the bottom edge of the cup. Spin the cup faster and faster until the marble rolls up the sides of the cup. Continue to spin the cup as you lift it off the table. The marble will continue rolling around inside the cup!

What's Happening?

Isaac Newton created several laws to describe how things move. The first law says that an object will keep moving in a straight line unless a force pushes or pulls on it. The marble rolls in a straight line, but the sides of the cup push it into a circle with a centripetal force. The sides of the cup slope just slightly outward, so the marble moves upward as it pushes out. If you keep the marble moving, it will stay inside the cup.

May Centripetal Force Be with You

This spinning coin trick defies the force of gravity!

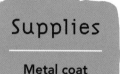

Supplies

Metal coat hanger, Quarter

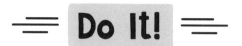

Do It!

1. Pull the bottom of the coat hanger out so that it changes from a triangle shape to a diamond shape. Hang the diamond on your finger so that the hanger is upside down. Bend the curved part of the handle so that the end is now straight up and flat on top.

2. Carefully balance the quarter on the end of the handle. This might take a couple of tries. With your finger through the top part of the diamond and the quarter balanced on the handle, gently swing the hanger back and forth. Do not make any sudden or jerky movements. Keep the motion smooth. Slowly increase the swings until you can swing the hanger all the way around. The quarter will stay on the end of the hanger handle!

What's Happening?

According to Isaac Newton, objects — such as quarters — keep moving in a straight line unless a force acts on them. In this case, the quarter is moving in a straight line and the coat hanger keeps pushing it in a circle. That force between the quarter and hanger, called centripetal force, is just enough to beat gravity if the coat hanger is moving. If you stop the hanger when the quarter is at the top of its swing, you will see it fall straight down.

What If?

What if you use a different coin? Try a dime, penny, and nickel. Do these coins work as well as the quarter?

Falling Mug

Do you trust physics? The fate of a coffee mug is in the balance!

Supplies

Coffee mug (one your grown-ups won't mind if it breaks), 30-inch piece of string, Metal teaspoon, Pencil, Pillows

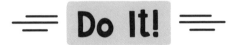
Do It!

1. Tie one end of the string to the spoon and the other end to the handle of the mug.

2. Hold the pencil straight out in one hand and put the string over the pencil so that the mug hangs just under the pencil.

3. Hold the spoon in the other hand and stretch it straight out across the pencil and away from the mug. When you are ready, let go of the spoon. Does the mug crash to the floor? Where does the spoon end up? The first time you do this trick, put some pillows on the floor just in case the mug hits the ground. After you get the hang of it, you can remove the pillows.

What's Happening?

If all goes as it should, the spoon will spin around the pencil and stop the mug from hitting the ground. When you let go of the spoon, gravity pulls it down and the string pulls it sideways. This causes the spoon to swing downward in an arc around the pencil. As the mug falls, it makes the string shorter. The shorter string causes the spoon to spin around the pencil faster and faster, just like when an ice skater brings their arms inward to spin faster. Eventually, the spoon wraps the string around the pencil and stops the mug from falling.

What If?

What if you use a longer string? You could use a string that is several feet long and stand on a ladder. How close does the mug get to the ground? Does the weight of the mug or the spoon matter? You can use washers, nuts, or other small objects instead of the mug and spoon to find the perfect set of light and heavy weights to make this trick work.

Balloon-kabob

Every great magician knows how to push a needle through a balloon.
Now you can too!

Supplies

Balloon (helium quality works best), Bamboo skewer, Petroleum jelly

== Do It! ==

1. Blow up the balloon and tie it off. Make sure the balloon is smaller than the bamboo skewer.

2. Rub a little petroleum jelly over the bamboo skewer. Take the pointy end of the skewer and hold it near the knot of the balloon where the balloon is just starting to stretch out. Push and twist the point of the skewer through the balloon. As soon as you break through the balloon, push the skewer in. If you hear a hissing sound, rub a little petroleum jelly around the skewer to seal the hole.

3. Turn the balloon over and find the dimple at the very top where the rubber is a little darker and not as stretched out. Again, twist and push the pointy end of the skewer until it comes out the other side of the balloon. You now have a balloon on a stick —or a balloon-kabob!

What's Happening?

Balloons are made of polymers, or chains of molecules. When you blow up the balloon, the polymer chains stretch and pull on each other but hold together. The key to getting a skewer through a balloon is to poke it between the polymer chains where they are not quite as stretched out — near the knot and on the top. Try poking the skewer through the side of the balloon where the polymer chains are stretched the most. The chains break and the balloon pops.

What If?

What if you could hold the polymer chains together? Place a piece of clear tape on the side of the balloon and try to poke a pin through it. What happens?

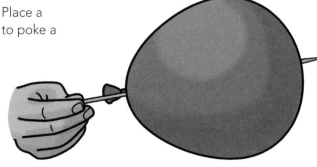

Index